Contemplation in the High Desert
Teresa E. Gallion

Contemplation

in the High Desert

Quatrains inspired by the Poetry of Rumi

by

Teresa E. Gallion

inner child press, ltd.

Contemplation in the High Desert
Teresa E. Gallion

Contemplation in the High Desert
Teresa E. Gallion

General Information

Contemplation in the High Desert

Author : Teresa E. Gallion

1st Edition : November, 2011

This Publishing is protected under Copyright Law as a "Collection". All rights for all submissions are retained by the Individual Artist and / or Poet. No part of this Publishing may be Reproduced, Transferred in any manner without the prior **WRITTEN CONSENT** of the "Material Owner" or it's Representative Inner Child Press.

Any such violation infringes upon the Creative and Intellectual Property of the Owner pursuant to International and Federal Copyright Law.

Any queries pertaining to this "Collection" should be addressed to Publisher of Record.

Publisher Information

1st Edition : Inner Child Press, Ltd.
innerchildpress@gmail.com
www.innerchildpress.com

This Collection is protected under U.S. and International Copyright Laws.

Copyright © 2011 : Teresa E. Gallion
Filed by : Inner Child Press, Ltd.

Library of Congress : 1-682481631

ISBN-13 : 978-0615557786

ISBN-10 : 0615557783

Cover Photo : Teresa E. Gallion
Cover Design : William S. Peters, Sr.
Interior Photo : Robin Neft

$ 16.95

Contemplation in the High Desert
Teresa E. Gallion

Contemplation in the High Desert
Teresa E. Gallion

Dedicated

to

Hertzog and Teresa Gallion

Two Loving Parents

Contemplation in the High Desert
Teresa E. Gallion

Contemplation in the High Desert
Teresa E. Gallion

Many thanks to

Debbi Brody

for keeping me grounded during the review and editing of this body of work.

Light and love to you my friend.

Teresa

Contemplation in the High Desert
Teresa E. Gallion

Contemplation in the High Desert
Teresa E. Gallion

Foreword

I like it when the musician, author or poet behind the words or music match in tone what I am reading or hearing in their work. I met Teresa before I heard her poetry, so learned that part first. She has a strong presence you can feel when she enters a room, and a gentle, velvety voice. Teresa is confident, grounded and earthy. She is a joy just to be with and laughs easily. I love it when she shares stories about her treks in the New Mexico mountains and desert and weaves the deep revelations that come as she hikes.

So as I read the quatrains in this book, and read lines like "I hear God laughing," or "Awakened to the Master's touch," or "Watching angels Spar in the velvet night," I know they have more meaning and realness than they would from anyone else. Teresa has actually *heard* God laughing. You can hear it in her own laughter as she stacks chairs with me after a worship service or a gig. She has indeed *awakened to her Master's touch*. It shows in her eyes and in the way she treats those around her.

When Teresa writes, "The truth stands / next to the blade of grass / it strokes your leg /every time you walk across my land," it is not simply a pretty poetic metaphor - she has *felt* both the blade of grass *and* the Truth standing next to her. She absolutely lives that way. And readers will know or sense this as they delve into these quatrains.

I have seen and felt the deep spirituality she lives and practices every day; she has read the works and teachings of Rumi for many years and exudes the same kind of genuine spiritual knowing. How honoring that her feet and mine walk the same dry, desert ground, and match in the spiritual and earthly energies. Yes, Teresa is my favorite kind of artist: one whose words are an extension of the Soul through which they emanate.

I invite you to take a spiritual journey in the pages that follow, inspired by the poetry of one whose words and being are one.

Michael John Hall
September, 2011

Contemplation in the High Desert
Teresa E. Gallion

Contemplation in the High Desert
Teresa E. Gallion

Preface

I am blessed to live in a high desert sanctuary where the sun shines more than 325 days a year, where the blue vaulted sky sports the most spectacular clouds and the night sky twinkles with ecstatic brilliance. Add to that the indescribably beautiful New Mexico landscape that draws artist and writers from all over the world. Within that context, I often find my head in the clouds whether walking the city streets, a desert arroyo or a Ponderosa Pine trail. For me, the New Mexico landscape is sacred ground. To share this space with the soul of Rumi is a blessing.

I became intimately acquainted with Rumi (13th century Sufi mystic and poet) over the past 12 years, sharing moments of quiet reading and reflection when one retreats from the tasks of daily living. Rumi resonates with my heart and soul as I sit in my rocking chair at home, as I sit by my morning campfire, as I sit in a natural hot spring in the mountains, as I sit by a river gently flowing past, as I sit under a Juniper Tree in the middle of the winter desert. No matter where I read Rumi, I am always inspired to write quatrains in response to the lyrics of wisdom that sing to me. He makes me laugh and cry, stand in righteous indignation, tremor with ecstatic joy and sometimes I dance, especially at home. All of these emotions flow into four line verses that respond to whatever touches me in that moment.

I did not start writing quatrains with the intent of publishing a book. My dear friend and colleague, Debbi Brody, would see a few of them every year when we attended the annual writers festival at Ghost Ranch Conference and Retreat Center in Northern New Mexico.

Contemplation in the High Desert
Teresa E. Gallion

Preface ... continued

She always said, "You need to put these together in a book." So I finally listened to that gentle nudge of Spirit coming through Debbi. When I put the quatrains together as a collection, I realized the significance of what I had been doing for so many years. I was unfolding spiritually at a pace I could handle. *Contemplation in the High Desert* has become a love offering to all who spend time in quiet reflection, contemplation or meditation. Each quatrain stands alone and may be used to start or end your day. If you are a writer, I hope it provides prompts to jump start your writing. If you are an artist, I hope it stimulates your creative juices. Regardless, I hope these quatrains stimulate your inner journey of self. Most of all, I hope they provide a partner to sit with and simply reflect on life.

I invite you to sit in a quiet space that gives you solace and taste the flavors of these quatrains. You may find some that will tickle your taste buds. The menu is diverse. Indulge yourself and may you find something that nourishes your Spirit.

Teresa E. Gallion
May the Blessings Be
September, 2011

Contemplation in the High Desert
Teresa E. Gallion

Table of Contents

Joy is earned	1
I break my bread	2
Listen to the harp	3
Undress your emotions	4
A river of joyfulness	5
Sitting by the stream	6
Burning in the fire	7
Soul floats down river	8
I sleep 24 hours	9
When you get knocked down	10
Every time you ask	11
Every tree that lies	12
Gratitude is misplaced	13
When snow and ice melt	14
Water is the history	15
The truth stands	16

Contemplation in the High Desert
Teresa E. Gallion

Table of Contents . . . continued

He listened	17
Sit beside the stream	18
I am the rosebud	19
The scent of light	20
Water rolls over	21
I saw you dance	22
I am full	23
Soul watches me	24
Your arms	25
I am hungry	26
The Beloved	27
Passion strolls in	28
To feel lonely	29
She said	30
The song of the waterfall	31
I lay a prayer	32

Contemplation in the High Desert
Teresa E. Gallion

Table of Contents . . . continued

Some days	33
She followed the Beloved	34
Look beyond the words	35
Karmic creditors	36
The master of knowledge	37
I lock onto its gaze	38
Lightning streaks	39
I move	40
I sit on planet earth	41
Spirit rubs ashes	42
This is your best	43
Rub my knees	44
Life's lessons	45
You already know	46
Truth manifests	47
He drank from the chalice	48

Contemplation in the High Desert
Teresa E. Gallion

Table of Contents . . . continued

I skip on the stars	49
I admit	50
I hugged the darkness	51
Death stopped at my gate	52
My tears ran away	53
Your words pierce	54
I was whipped	55
Tsunami broke my silence	56
The desert is enchanted	57
I trotted into friendship	58
I tasted human love	59
Sitting on this desert mesa	60
Cotton candy and hot dogs	61
She is sweet wine	62
Touch me	63
I have a hangover	64

Contemplation in the High Desert
Teresa E. Gallion

Table of Contents . . . continued

If you look	65
When someone reminds you	66
Sugar rolls down	67
I sat submerged	68
I thought of you	69
The blue light	70
The loss of love	71
Red wine spills	72
We exchanged hands	73
I lay beside the fireplace	74
A thought of you	75
Lapis streaks	76
I stared down a wolf	77
Black rubber stains	78
I take a handful of sky	79
I awake to morning	80

Contemplation in the High Desert
Teresa E. Gallion

Table of Contents . . . continued

Drink from my river	81
A choir of angels	82
The first light	83
A seeker came	84
God touched her	85
The gentle breeze	86
She panics	87
The seeker runs around	88
Wake up, wake up	89
The spiritual fire	90
I have no expectations	91
I cannot tell you	92
I play with her	93
He raped her	94
Step lightly	95
Give me a cool drink	96

Contemplation in the High Desert
Teresa E. Gallion

Table of Contents . . . continued

A dove lands	97
Plant seeds	98
The eyes of the wolf	99
When you are weary	100
Give me a bowl of strawberries	101
I want to touch your petals	102
A picture weaves	103
The door is open	104
I see you gazing	105
Here in the desert silence	106
Rise up, come fly with me	107
Looking into the void	108
I climb the side	109
The sky is falling	110
I ate apples	111
His inner child	112

Contemplation in the High Desert
Teresa E. Gallion

Table of Contents . . . continued

Opened my heart	113
Looking inward	114
I taste a wisdom cherry	115
There is a message	116
A full moon rises	117
Life giving water flows	118
I walk the desert	119
We ride	120
Come to me	121
Greed walks boldly	122
New Mexico sunsets	123
Endorsements	**125 - 129**

Contemplation in the High Desert
Teresa E. Gallion

Contemplation in the High Desert
Teresa E. Gallion

Contemplation in the High Desert
Teresa E. Gallion

Contemplation

in the High Desert

Quatrains inspired by the Poetry of Rumi

by

Teresa E. Gallion

inner child press, ltd.

Contemplation in the High Desert
Teresa E. Gallion

Contemplation in the High Desert
Teresa E. Gallion

Joy is earned in charitable deeds
If you are not joyful
You have much work to do
Go across the street and help your neighbor pull
weeds

Contemplation in the High Desert
Teresa E. Gallion

I break my bread in half
Hand a piece to Spirit
Spirit gives it back to me
Share with your brothers and sisters

Contemplation in the High Desert
Teresa E. Gallion

Listen to the harp play in the garden
The melody reaches for your heart
A rainbow of strings
Are tuned to your consciousness

Contemplation in the High Desert
Teresa E. Gallion

Undress your emotions
Bathe them in this stream
Feel the power of the sacred water
Dress you in love

Contemplation in the High Desert
Teresa E. Gallion

A river of joyfulness
Floats in the light and sound
Sit in solitude with the master
Get acquainted with joy

Contemplation in the High Desert
Teresa E. Gallion

Sitting by the stream
I hear God laughing
Ecstatic wind massages my face
Soul dances in the sunlight

Contemplation in the High Desert
Teresa E. Gallion

Burning in the fire of love
We surrender to the moment
Spirit offers a ride
We fly on the wings of butterflies

Contemplation in the High Desert
Teresa E. Gallion

Soul floats down river
Bathing in light and sound
The experience of freedom
Is imprinted on the heart

Contemplation in the High Desert
Teresa E. Gallion

I sleep 24 hours per day
And life bounces all around me
But today I drink at the well of purification
Awakened to the Master's touch

Contemplation in the High Desert
Teresa E. Gallion

When you get knocked down hard
Lick your boots clean
Get up
Start walking again

Contemplation in the High Desert
Teresa E. Gallion

Every time you ask for help from Spirit
An answer comes
Not necessarily the way you want it
Always as a healing massage

Contemplation in the High Desert
Teresa E. Gallion

Every tree that lies down in the forest
Is a sacrifice to earth
A return to its origin
The beginning of rebirth

Contemplation in the High Desert
Teresa E. Gallion

Gratitude is misplaced
In outward proclamation
From the heart's landscape
It flows freely

Contemplation in the High Desert
Teresa E. Gallion

When snow and ice melt
Waters of life form
A pure lake for your heart
To float unattached

Contemplation in the High Desert
Teresa E. Gallion

Water is the history
Of my soul flowing past
Through the current
Many passages

Contemplation in the High Desert
Teresa E. Gallion

The truth stands
Next to the blade of grass
It strokes your leg
Every time you walk across my land

Contemplation in the High Desert
Teresa E. Gallion

He listened very attentively
Then asked, *do you see the solitary branch*
Focus on the tip
Discipline will show you the way

Contemplation in the High Desert
Teresa E. Gallion

Sit beside the stream
To gather your thoughts
Bend your knees toward the ripples
Feel the presence of God

Contemplation in the High Desert
Teresa E. Gallion

I am the rosebud that tempts your nose
I am the harp string of your heart
I am the musical growl in your belly
I am the mystical massage on your cheeks

Contemplation in the High Desert
Teresa E. Gallion

The scent of light
Touches intimately
A slow melt in the sand
Releases body from soul

Contemplation in the High Desert
Teresa E. Gallion

Water rolls over the falls
The rush of spirit
Grabs attention
Expands smiles

Contemplation in the High Desert
Teresa E. Gallion

I saw you dance under the light bulb
It shimmered above your head
What power you have
Stepping to the Beloved's rhythm

Contemplation in the High Desert
Teresa E. Gallion

I am full
Yet the light penetrates
There is always
Room for God's holy light

Contemplation in the High Desert
Teresa E. Gallion

Soul watches me all night
At daybreak kisses my forehead
Steps back into my body
With a cup of gratitude to share

Contemplation in the High Desert
Teresa E. Gallion

Your arms are the tree trunks
My hands cling to
If I let go
I have to face life

Contemplation in the High Desert
Teresa E. Gallion

I am hungry
Watching angels
Spar in the velvet night
I want a piece of that action

Contemplation in the High Desert
Teresa E. Gallion

The Beloved sits at the river bank
Relieving hearts of pain and sorrow
I think I will sit at the river
Wait for my turn to surrender

Contemplation in the High Desert
Teresa E. Gallion

Passion strolls in on a slow breeze
Flirts with everything in its path
If I miss its crimson kiss
I will not be bound to earth school

Contemplation in the High Desert
Teresa E. Gallion

To feel lonely is a failure to see
All the gifts that surround you
Open your eyes
The world waits for your embrace

Contemplation in the High Desert
Teresa E. Gallion

She said, *your head is in the clouds*
I said, *pure joy, wonderful pillow*
She said, *don't play with me*
I said, *let's dance with the Beloved*

Contemplation in the High Desert
Teresa E. Gallion

The song of the waterfall
Entertains day walkers
Arms bent backwards
In meditative pose

Contemplation in the High Desert
Teresa E. Gallion

I lay a prayer on your chest
To soothe your burning sleep
It is selfish to hold back
When love flows in my river

Contemplation in the High Desert
Teresa E. Gallion

Some days it is enough
To simply look up
Take a deep breadth
Savor the deep blue sky

Contemplation in the High Desert
Teresa E. Gallion

She followed the Beloved to the garden
He touched a rose
With a loving thought
Her smile expanded like a waterfall

Contemplation in the High Desert
Teresa E. Gallion

Look beyond the words
Catch a glimpse of the tsunami
Crowding the shoreline
Planting seeds of love in mayhem

Contemplation in the High Desert
Teresa E. Gallion

Karmic creditors come to collect
I bend over my altar to dry my tears
I am gently picked up
Anointed with the blue light of love

Contemplation in the High Desert
Teresa E. Gallion

The master of knowledge spoke to me without a
word
He unveiled the stage show on the planet
Raised his hand and said
Behold! Be silent!

Contemplation in the High Desert
Teresa E. Gallion

I lock onto its gaze
My body floats to its ship
Running up and down the deck
I stumble into the presence of Spirit

Contemplation in the High Desert
Teresa E. Gallion

Lightning streaks across the sky
God speaks with authority
I bow in respect
I lived through the experience

Contemplation in the High Desert
Teresa E. Gallion

I move from wanting to longing
To hear your voice say my name
Thoughts of you cast a shadow
On the path I walk

Contemplation in the High Desert
Teresa E. Gallion

I sit on planet earth
Spell bound in illusion
Forgetfulness threatens me
Slows my journey home

Contemplation in the High Desert
Teresa E. Gallion

Spirit rubs ashes of life across his face
Karma drips from his cheeks
The River swells in red
Steam climbs skyward pulls Soul along

Contemplation in the High Desert
Teresa E. Gallion

This is your best moment
Yesterday is memory
Tomorrow is not yours
Breathe gratitude in the present moment

Contemplation in the High Desert
Teresa E. Gallion

Rub my knees to the bone
Spirit releases its protective grip
I want to run up the side of the mountain
And proclaim my freedom

Contemplation in the High Desert
Teresa E. Gallion

Life's lessons line your pockets
They overflow with spiritual treasures
Jiggle your pockets
Be grateful for the coins of wisdom

Contemplation in the High Desert
Teresa E. Gallion

You already know the answers
When you are ready
Just look inside
Soul holds them with open arms

Contemplation in the High Desert
Teresa E. Gallion

Truth manifests in the light
Are you ready to ride the light stream
Back home to God
Release old body and let Soul fly

Contemplation in the High Desert
Teresa E. Gallion

He drank from the chalice
Gold ran down his cheeks
The elixir of Spirit massaged his body
Teasing Soul to pursue the chase

Contemplation in the High Desert
Teresa E. Gallion

I skip on the stars
Hug the moon close to my heart
I am blessed
I surrender to bliss

Contemplation in the High Desert
Teresa E. Gallion

I admit
Your rejection struck a painful nerve
Thank you for waking me up
I fell asleep on the path

Contemplation in the High Desert
Teresa E. Gallion

I hugged the darkness
Cuddled my pain
Wept all my gratitude
At the feet of Spirit

Contemplation in the High Desert
Teresa E. Gallion

Death stopped at my gate
Saw your light in my window
Death ran from life
Tucking its tail in the wind

Contemplation in the High Desert
Teresa E. Gallion

My tears ran away
Looking for a place to hide
You walked into my life
Holding my bucket of tears

Contemplation in the High Desert
Teresa E. Gallion

Your words pierce my heart
The pain so intense
I hug it in your honor
Peace floods my veins

Contemplation in the High Desert
Teresa E. Gallion

I was whipped by your rejection
Refused the grief strutting in
Bent over my river of tears
Thanked the Beloved for the experience

Contemplation in the High Desert
Teresa E. Gallion

Tsunami broke my silence
Made me look up
into the window of truth
I wanted to run and hide

Contemplation in the High Desert
Teresa E. Gallion

The desert is enchanted
Calls forth my longing
Rising from the sand
As I engage the moment

Contemplation in the High Desert
Teresa E. Gallion

I trotted into friendship
Like a royal white stallion
Friendship rejected me
Did not break my spirit

Contemplation in the High Desert
Teresa E. Gallion

I tasted human love
In the kiss on your lips
The honey melting your embrace
Reminded me of home

Contemplation in the High Desert
Teresa E. Gallion

Sitting on this desert mesa
Watching Pedernal suck clouds for dinner
I am enthralled by the natural power
Of nature's simplicity

Footnote : Pedernal is a mountain in northern New Mexico

Contemplation in the High Desert
Teresa E. Gallion

Cotton candy and hot dogs on a stick
Riding decades of change
Hold their position
On the rotating axis of earth

Contemplation in the High Desert
Teresa E. Gallion

She is sweet wine hugging my tongue
Vermillion butterflies land on my lip
To taste the sweetness
Of an unknown goddess

Contemplation in the High Desert
Teresa E. Gallion

Touch me in intimate places
And hug me in eternal bliss
For you bring me joy
That is sweet and pure.

Contemplation in the High Desert
Teresa E. Gallion

I have a hangover from loving you
That sleep will not cure
Don't get caught like me
Run like hell for the mountains

Contemplation in the High Desert
Teresa E. Gallion

If you look at the mountain
And laughter fills your belly
Share your insight
With a lost and lonely friend

Contemplation in the High Desert
Teresa E. Gallion

When someone reminds you
How emotional you are
Remember the healing wisdom of Spirit
Comes in subtle ways

Contemplation in the High Desert
Teresa E. Gallion

Sugar rolls down your lips
I lick the clouds with authority
That is as close as I may come to you
We were separated at birth

Contemplation in the High Desert
Teresa E. Gallion

I sat submerged in mud
Soaked the misery from my bones
You extended your hand
I stood up, embraced an ecstatic wind

Contemplation in the High Desert
Teresa E. Gallion

I thought of you
A butterfly landed on the window
My heart fluttered
As I scanned your wings

Contemplation in the High Desert
Teresa E. Gallion

The blue light soared above me
All sorrows melted like butter
My spirit took flight
In the hands of the Beloved

Contemplation in the High Desert
Teresa E. Gallion

The loss of love trotted behind me
As I tried to out run the wind
There's something tight in grief and pain
That gives us strength to run

Contemplation in the High Desert
Teresa E. Gallion

Red wine spills from his lips
Infuses life in the plants tickling his feet
They rise
Filled with laughter and love

Contemplation in the High Desert
Teresa E. Gallion

We exchanged hands today
I gave you my left hand
You gave me your right hand
Everything changed for the better

Contemplation in the High Desert
Teresa E. Gallion

I lay beside the fireplace
Burning with joy and peace
I want to run away from responsibility
And dance in the flames of love

Contemplation in the High Desert
Teresa E. Gallion

A thought of you so powerful
It breaks my wine glass
I cannot afford such thoughts
Crystal is too expensive

Contemplation in the High Desert
Teresa E. Gallion

Lapis streaks between the clouds
Birds flap wings above earth, below sky
A mirage of light
Floods the atmosphere

Contemplation in the High Desert
Teresa E. Gallion

I stared down a wolf
Claiming the edge of the forest
This is not the first time
Courage has dominated my life

Contemplation in the High Desert
Teresa E. Gallion

Black rubber stains the concrete
The street buckles under the pain
The next tire challenges the road
Tread melts into liquid distress

Contemplation in the High Desert
Teresa E. Gallion

I take a handful of sky
Toss it to a friend
Watch it swell like an ocean wave
Around her heart

Contemplation in the High Desert
Teresa E. Gallion

I awake to morning lying in dead skin
Shed on the dark night of soul
Skin breathing love and gratitude
My new dress code

Contemplation in the High Desert
Teresa E. Gallion

Drink from my river
It is pure and sweet
I know this to be true
I saw the Beloved playing in the water

Contemplation in the High Desert
Teresa E. Gallion

A choir of angels sings
At the foot of my bed
My guardian says, *come with me*
It is time to face the music

Contemplation in the High Desert
Teresa E. Gallion

The first light of morning
Hugs me gently
Opens the pathway
On the trail to the Beloved's cabin

Contemplation in the High Desert
Teresa E. Gallion

A seeker came to the river
Saw the Beloved fishing
He asked, *why are you fishing*
So that you may eat

Contemplation in the High Desert
Teresa E. Gallion

God touched her with a thought
She could not stop laughing
A boat appeared in the water
God said, *come ride with me*

Contemplation in the High Desert
Teresa E. Gallion

The gentle breeze
Knows the secrets of the forest
Listen with your heart
Embrace the storyteller

Contemplation in the High Desert
Teresa E. Gallion

She panics at the crossroad
Unable to move
A stranger appears on the road
He says, *all roads lead to God*

Contemplation in the High Desert
Teresa E. Gallion

The seeker runs around the forest like a madman
The teacher walks casually in the forest
The seeker yells, *where can I find God*
The teacher says, *you're standing on sacred ground*

Contemplation in the High Desert
Teresa E. Gallion

Wake up, wake up
The Beloved stands at your window
Waiting for you
To come out to play

Contemplation in the High Desert
Teresa E. Gallion

The spiritual fire burns within
It is love
Open the gates of illumination
Let the flames hijack a ride in the trees

Contemplation in the High Desert
Teresa E. Gallion

I have no expectations
I want to give you a gift
A love offering from soul
My smile

Contemplation in the High Desert
Teresa E. Gallion

I cannot tell you how to live your life
I can only tell you how I live mine
Is there something from my dinner plate you need
Take a spoonful please

Contemplation in the High Desert
Teresa E. Gallion

I play with her in the yard
Whose teeth are strongest in this sock tugging war
My dog does not care
She is in dog heaven playing with her master

Contemplation in the High Desert
Teresa E. Gallion

He raped her with words
Walked away licking his lips
Don't worry about his arrogance
Karma is coming to kick his butt

Contemplation in the High Desert
Teresa E. Gallion

Step lightly on this sacred ground
Like a baby's first steps
Tip toe into awakening
From the Beloved's touch

Contemplation in the High Desert
Teresa E. Gallion

Give me a cool drink of water
From the palm of your hand
Your soft touch
Fills me with gratitude

Contemplation in the High Desert
Teresa E. Gallion

A dove lands on the ground
Lays an olive branch at her feet
He walks in armored
With a dozen red roses

Contemplation in the High Desert
Teresa E. Gallion

Plant seeds of delight
In the garden of ecstasy
Watch the birds come to steal
To plant seeds of love in mayhem

Contemplation in the High Desert
Teresa E. Gallion

The eyes of the wolf
Lock my gaze
Pierces my inner child
With stains of love

Contemplation in the High Desert
Teresa E. Gallion

When you are weary and restless
Get off the negative road
Step knee deep into a mud ditch
Pretend you are stomping grapes

Contemplation in the High Desert
Teresa E. Gallion

Give me a bowl of strawberries
A love offering from your heart
I will hold the sweetness
Close to my soul

Contemplation in the High Desert
Teresa E. Gallion

I want to touch your petals
Feel your velvet charms
Massage my fingers
Into a precious ruby

Contemplation in the High Desert
Teresa E. Gallion

A picture weaves an intricate web
Stained with time memorials
Do we dare say
Open wide and let your children enter

Contemplation in the High Desert
Teresa E. Gallion

The door is open
Come into my house
Drink from my fountain of peace
Enfold your Spirit in love

Contemplation in the High Desert
Teresa E. Gallion

I see you gazing into sadness
Your tears flood the road
I extend my hand
To help you climb out of loneliness

Contemplation in the High Desert
Teresa E. Gallion

Here in the desert silence
I find sanctuary
Here in the desert silence
I hear the hum of sacred voices

Contemplation in the High Desert
Teresa E. Gallion

Rise up, come fly with me
I float in beauty
Surrounded by light and sound
I am love

Contemplation in the High Desert
Teresa E. Gallion

Looking into the void
Heavenly light draws me to you
Touch my hand Oh Beloved
I want to float in eternal bliss

Contemplation in the High Desert
Teresa E. Gallion

I climb the side of your back
Touch the jewels running up your spine
Feel the presence of Spirit
Guiding all hikers up the trail

Contemplation in the High Desert
Teresa E. Gallion

The sky is falling into my hands
Earth trembles on my behalf
My angel helps me hold the sky
In the palm of my hand

Contemplation in the High Desert
Teresa E. Gallion

I ate apples of peace
You sliced apples of joy
An apple slice touched your lips
Became an apple of love

Contemplation in the High Desert
Teresa E. Gallion

His inner child does hard drugs
Makes him run wild in the streets
Chasing the roaming dust
From the Beloved's feet

Contemplation in the High Desert
Teresa E. Gallion

Opened my heart
To nature's gallery
Swell of joy inexpressible
Ran wild across the landscape

Contemplation in the High Desert
Teresa E. Gallion

Looking inward
The light greets me
When I reach for it
Radiance blooms in my hands

Contemplation in the High Desert
Teresa E. Gallion

I taste a wisdom cherry
The garden in my heart blooms
I run across the universe
Sharing love bouquets

Contemplation in the High Desert
Teresa E. Gallion

There is a message
In the jaws of the flames
Buckle up homo sapiens
I am pissed off

Contemplation in the High Desert
Teresa E. Gallion

A full moon rises
Teasing the heart valves
A cascade of radiant light
Calls me home

Contemplation in the High Desert
Teresa E. Gallion

Life giving water flows over the waterfall
Evaporates in a flowing mist
I must acquire a thirst
To catch that eternal wave

Contemplation in the High Desert
Teresa E. Gallion

I walk the desert
Lifetime after lifetime
And today I found
The Beloved's footprints in the sand

Contemplation in the High Desert
Teresa E. Gallion

We ride the white stallions of joy
Galloping in ecstatic bliss
God kissed us
In the shadow of the trees

Contemplation in the High Desert
Teresa E. Gallion

Come to me
Let me melt your sorrows
In the purification pools
Only awakened souls may enter

Contemplation in the High Desert
Teresa E. Gallion

Greed walks boldly
Down city streets
Eats all weakness
That crosses its path

Contemplation in the High Desert
Teresa E. Gallion

New Mexico sunsets
Make my lips smack
Like delicious food
Give me an extra helping please

Contemplation in the High Desert
Teresa E. Gallion

Contemplation in the High Desert
Teresa E. Gallion

Endorsements

Contemplation in the High Desert
Teresa E. Gallion

Contemplation in the High Desert
Teresa E. Gallion

Debbi Brody

I have been reading Teresa Gallion's poetry for over a decade. It is persistently fresh, lyrical, insightful and without an ounce of pretension. Her understanding of spirit and its role in our every day lives, as well as in the natural world, lends an uplifting sense of light to all Ms. Gallion gathers into words.

Debbi Brody
Poet, Poetry Educator
Author of *Portraits in Poetry* and *FreeForm*

Jane Vincent Taylor

The High Desert is a thin place where consciousness touches other times and older voices. Teresa's quatrains honor the inner and outer landscape where transformation is both common and wondrous. Rumi swirls through her poems and we, too, are invited to walk in the desert with the Beloved.

Jane Vincent Taylor
Poet

Contemplation in the High Desert
Teresa E. Gallion

Lou Liberty

We are greatly fortunate that Teresa Gallion has been in conversation with Rumi for several years. We are even more fortunate that she has decided to share those deeply personal quatrain conversations with us through her book, *Contemplation in the High Desert*.

Teresa's work is profoundly spiritual, as we would expect since she is inspired by the mystical poet, Rumi. She is not a copyist, however. Teresa's poems record her own seeking and therefore they carry the fresh intimacy of conversation with a best friend. More importantly, her work goes beyond self to Self in its exploration.

Teresa's quatrains are that wonderful paradox of tangibility and the transcendent. Her first quatrain reminds us that if we are seeking joy, we must be charitable. Accomplishing that task may be as simple as her instruction to us, "Go across the street and help your neighbor pull weeds".

The remaining quatrains carry us through diverse moments, moods, and experiences, each one bearing a gift of insight, a rare sip of that "wine" that so enchanted Rumi and likewise all who seek Spirit.

From philosophic to erotic, from to courageous to playful to profound, *Contemplation in the High Desert* takes us on a mystical journey in a free flowing, thoughtful, engaging way. We arrive at the end of the trip laden with treasure.

Lou Liberty
Author, Poet, Fellow Traveler
www.louliberty.net

Contemplation in the High Desert
Teresa E. Gallion

Jeanine Hathaway

Teresa Gallion writes out of the authority of her own experience: of joy, of surrender, sacrifice and growl. The contrasts, say, between the High Desert and waterfalls, the edge of a forest and sorrow that melts like butter, are both unexpected and apt. Each brief quatrain offers treasures for our culture which seems too focused on scarcity. Each quatrain is a gift, "a coin of wisdom," from a writer whose generosity is lavish.

Jeanine Hathaway
Author
The Ex-Nun Poems
The Self as Constellation
Motherhouse

Gary Stewart Chorre'

Teresa Gallion has been a stalwart contributor to the Albuquerque poetry scene for many years. It is both as a friend and admirer that I joyously took the time to peruse her Quatrains for this book. While short in length, each literary gem provoked introspective rumination, igniting an epiphany of awareness that illuminates a particular interaction or personality trait leading to that "Aha" moment of understanding. Hers, is the clear light of wisdom sparkling bright and true in the glint of a poetic insight only the few possess.

Gary Stewart Chorre'
Poet, Actor

Contemplation in the High Desert
Teresa E. Gallion

Gregory L. Candela

Teresa Gallion is a well-known, highly-respected and beloved New Mexican poet. She is an avid hiker, and her poetry is inspired by the state's deserts, mountains and rivers. Her poetic landscapes are vast, compressed then powerfully released in the 4-line poems of *Contemplation in the High Desert*.

Gallion's meditations speak directly to her readers. She is their personal and passionate guide. Her poems are both imperative and welcoming :

> The truth stands
> Next to the blade of grass
> It strokes your leg
> Every time you walk across my land

With few exceptions, her quatrains have no regular rhythm or rhyme; however, the poet addresses her readers through dominate stressed (trochaic) and double-stressed (spondaic) syllables :

> Sit beside the stream
> To gather your thoughts
> Bend your knees toward the ripples
> Feel the presence of God

Half these poems command and invite; half confess—all reveal a wide-open spirit seeking spirit; all are spoken as Teresa Gallion speaks: forcefully, truly and beautifully.

Gregory L. Candela
Poet
Professor Emeritus, University of New Mexico

Contemplation in the High Desert
Teresa E. Gallion

~ fini ~

www.ingramcontent.com/pod-product-compliance
Lightning Source LLC
Chambersburg PA
CBHW071722090426
42738CB00009B/1852